The Present State of the Garden

The
Present State
of the
Garden

Heather Sellers

Lynx House Press

Spokane, Washington

ACKNOWLEDGMENTS

My thanks to John Brehm, Silvia Curbelo, Shari Ellis, Hunt Hawkins, Allyson Hoffman, A. Van Jordan, Phyllis McEwan, Kate LeSar, Robin Messing, Antwon Montgomery, Heide Nelson, Gianna Russo, Elaine Sexton, Enid Shomer, Elaine Smith, Kim Turner, and Helen Wallace. I'm grateful to my colleagues in the writing program at University of South Florida and to the University. Thanks also to Christopher Howell and the staff of Lynx House Press.

I'm grateful to the editors at the following journals, some in earlier versions:

Agni: "Accidental Practitioners"
Five Points: "Bush Gardens," "Dear Wolf," "Feed the Soil," "Present State of the Garden"
The Carolina Quarterly: "After My Mother Died"
Southern Poetry Review: "Aubade," "Poor Neighbors"
The Sun Magazine: "Unloose," "After He Left," "After Taking Me to Meet Great Aunt Fayrene"
The Bellingham Review: "Elegy With Plant-Sitter"
Image: "Beauty"
Prairie Schooner: "After Class"

"Interstate Four Ode" appears in *Dive,* a chapbook published by Yellow Jacket Press in 2014.

FIRST EDITION

Cover Art: Kevin Sloan.
Author Photo: Marina Kiriakou.
Book and Cover Design: Christine Holbert.

LYNX HOUSE PRESS books are distributed by the University of Washington Press, 4333 Brooklyn Avenue NE, Seattle, WA 98195-9570.

LIBRARY OF CONGRESS CATALOGING-IN-PUBLICATION DATA
is available from the Library of Congress.
ISBN 978-0-89924-180-7

CONTENTS

PART II

WE'RE ALREADY LOSING LIGHT

Late afternoon blue-gold
curtains over a pink sky.
A tropical plate, pecans.
The white rain, frittering
hibiscus. I would walk miles
for this perfume: these lemon
blossoms and your friendship.
I cannot tell you about my first
marriage or my father.
We're already losing light.

PART I

BUSH GARDENS

When I was a girl we drove the Plymouth,
a cream beige house of car across Florida,
old seabed still gleaming, sandy cattle ranches,
particular egrets, lattice trailer parks,
the Green Swamp's black water shining back
the world's oldest dreams.
Jeweled necklaces of cypress stood along the seams
between sand and liquid. Live oaks' long low limbs hovered
over the road, godly arms: *You are held,*
little family, held after all by something
greater than you will ever see.
We really never went anywhere.
But on this day my father drove, destination Tampa,
leaning back as though seated on a sofa, smoking
cigarettes. My mother, her eyes closed
in the front seat, shaded her face with her palms:
You're too close. Paul, you're following too close.
I didn't see any cars or problems
or into the future when we'd never
drive again to an American attraction.
I saw a crushed turtle, its blood a red
painting on pavement. I saw a red-tailed hawk
hung up in a pine and buzzards like preachers
nodding slow yes. I lay on the hot vinyl
back seat in shorts and a pink gingham
blouse and watched roseate spoonbills streak pink
lines across the blue felt sky. Telephone wires
insistent as music and Johnny Cash
a scratch of low desire on the radio.

At Busch Gardens when we walked through the gates
I expected a kingdom of shrubbery.
I knew a few bushes back home
and knew them as rooms in mansions,
mysterious branched havens
for storing brokenness, bird nests, creation myths,
dead dolls, other wrong and headless shames.
Once, in a park downtown,
I'd come across a man's underwear
in a bush, on its secret ground.
Was there anything a bush could not become?
I could live by myself in a bush. If it came to that.

Palm trees, kiosks, the beer hall, tinny carts, hot dogs,
plastic alligators with yellow sales tags
hung around their necks like amulets.
We walked across burning pavement so hot
lines wavered before us as in cartoons.
Not one bush in sight, not anywhere.
We boarded a shrunken steam train, toy red.
An incomprehensible man
in a safari suit narrated the Serengeti
over a speaker so scritchy, I covered my ears.
The gardens seemed at the border
between my family and the rest of the world.
I scanned the savannahs,
giraffes, elephants, impala, grateful
to my parents for setting me free.
At the next stop—an ocelot was promised—
I would hop down from the steam train,
duck under the fence, leap the gully,
enter my life.

UNLOOSE

After fifth grade, summer of the green one-piece,
I waited out front of the YMCA, downtown
Orlando, when a man on a motorcycle pulled up
under the portico where my mother collected me.
I lived in the swimsuit as skin. Barefoot
on the hot concrete, for the first time
I saw how a man could have been once a boy.
This was the day I didn't step away or go back inside
because I was afraid and not knowing
something significantly altering.
He had water-blue eyes, a long beard, no shirt,
and jeans I knew to be "bell-bottoms," but they had
no bells. His body was muscle smooth,
like a horse. Those pants had seams running
down the center of the legs. Useless seams.
I could feel my finger wanting to . . .
Finger! I put it in my mouth. I put a second finger
in, like a baby. He held his helmet in his arm,
like a football. "Hi," I said. But I meant
Can I ride? I meant around the parking lot. I meant
sit on the bike for one minute. I meant *I don't have
the kind of mother you might think I have.* (Where was my mother?)
I felt wings grow out of my back from the straps
of the green suit. I stepped toward his motorcycle,
stepped out of my story. I only wanted to prove that
I wasn't afraid, wasn't like her. He said, "No, it's hot!"
too late. I'd already pressed my knee against the silver pipe.
I heard the fizzle, the spit, felt the bright pain and the shame.
On my skin that afternoon is still with me, the hard heart of scar,
the beginning of the girl in two pieces.

WET SEASON

The Little Manatee River cuts
Florida almost clean in half,
a clear, deep and open vein
rushing to the Gulf.
Just married, a dawn start,
he and I were on the river,
canoe lashed to the bending
willow like lug work,
the slender silver dented, a rented
thing holding a tender thing,
new and right and good.
We were not yet in over our heads.
He recited something from memory
in languishing southern syllables
and the racket of our aluminum
banged the low branches, accompanying.
I was mostly listening.
I did not feel the sting.
I did not feel anything
puncture my skin.
I'd draped my arms
on the gun whales,
feeling strong and wanted by the world
on the clear and rushing river.
The current broke around our craft
in the tricky spackled shades
I half-heard his words.
I listened to the invisible
songbirds, listened to the rhythm
of the tug of our cord.
The water was clear all the way down

to the ancient white river bed.
When is fast-moving anything
this clear? We'd had so much
rain early May, the watermark rose
high up the waists of loblollies
on the banks. A week earlier
the great storm reversed the river.
We would have drowned here
under twelve stories of water.
After we undid ourselves
and drifting, I leaned over
to examine the black
bulbous fish, barbed bottom-feeders,
so many, too many—dozens
of dumb dull lumps
stationed on the river bed
as we paddled quickly now—
the canoe soon due.
I wanted to be not so
against proliferation.
What were these fish
who do not swim, only hover,
commas on the white sand,
motionless in the liquid?
When I woke that night—
still in love
with all we did not know—
I woke burning, the red blister
on my inner thigh, a weird square,
like a box, a stinging brand.

He took such care with the skin
and whispered, as though I were a child
or there were children sleeping:
Something venomous.
What could have found me
in such a tender place
without my knowing?
I remembered my skirt in the boat,
how I felt like a flower
at the prow, all come-hither,
in my paradise.

AFTER LOVE

The thing no one ever tells you about joy
is that it has very little real pleasure in it.

—*Zadie Smith*

We lay side-by-side on the bed.
How non-self reigned in all the rooms!
And the joy in knowing parts of us
that can't ever be known:
Isn't love a religion that way?
And the act turns out to be a sacrament
after all, as promised and not as promised.
Witness likewise the wedding of evening to night,
preparation for a Sunday meal at home
with regular things, the taking, tending
and putting away of plates, cloth
and flatware, all completed
in one unbroken motion.
Two don't actually become one.
But bodies together thus—mirror and pavilion—
well, it almost feels like wisdom.

SOMETIMES, AFTER

He disappeared into the bathroom.
And in the violent light
I sat on the counter like a girl.
I watched him work his washcloth,
the former nurse, undoing what we'd done.
I watched him brush.
I watched him to be more with him,
to feel every bristle.
He was a very thorough brusher.
I watched reversed-him in the mirror.
I watched actual him
scrubbing his teeth inside his grimace.
I watched her watch him,
how each one had another,
two togethers endlessly doubled.
When he was asleep
I lay awake
with many thoughts like petals,
and many thoughts on rivers
carrying strand after strand of empty canoes.

AUBADE

We dawdled as kinglets
in the kitchen when morning came to us,
birdsong and bright light in stereo,
husband at the stove working
the frayed spatula, my mother's.
How every morning he tended
the edges, tucked the eggs, gently turning
another lopsided holy spill
into a pillow.
So too was I cared for,
frizzled parts tucked away
and no longer mattering so,
broken and open self-thing
safe in the pocket of marriage.
He could have fed me anything
when we bade morning
come to us.

POOR NEIGHBORS

How well the worldwide warmth
clung to us as we walked after breakfast
with guidebooks like hunters, like children, like birds
intent on finding something new
to name and love and light on.
This morning: gold-brown rotting fruit
on the streets. I leaned on him
as we fingered the slippery seeds,
hypnotized. He read aloud from the pages:
Toxic! Edible! Which parts?
I interrupted to rename him
fake Latin names, to describe the fruits of him
in studious glorious guidebook syntax,
relevant features and mating predilections,
his sweetest blossom time.
Against the backdrop of morning bird bright
I don't think we ever stopped talking
as we walked down the street
each morning with the guidebook
held high, like a bible, which it is,
intent on knowing by naming
every living thing.
Binocular-slung, traffic-oblivious, job-averse,
with dirty breakfast dishes at home,
crusting in the sink in the sun,
grown man and grown woman
living as children, collecting bugs and seeds,
lost in the crown of the specimen.
We have a match!

STRANDED

They depend on
us, my mother said, of men.
They are weak, men.
They can't be kept, men.
Did the men
belong to us?
Try to
keep your man.
Never leave a man.
Never let him go.
Do not depend on men.

Mother, I can show you
the pressure of erasure,
my rising, its pink madness.
I can show you
still bones, charcoal
bones and a girl
in a house
in a world where men
did what they wanted
and we did what
they wanted.

I was so afraid of her.

AFTER TAKING ME TO MEET GREAT AUNT FAYRENE

Darkness lowered as we drove
across town, back to your childhood
home. Your father at the counter banged his knife.
What do you see in him? He said to me of you.
The boy's no good. Not good for anything.
I held your hand and doubled
myself and said, *He is good.*
No one said another word.
Your mother said dinner was ready.
She hoped it was good brisket. She was not sure. Food's changed.
A Western resounded in the background.
Your father repeated
That boy's no-good no good. A way of putting words
together as weaponry. A joke not-joke.
The house smelled of meat. You washed
your hands. I wondered how you took it and
what we would speak of regarding your father.
Then the phone was ringing. Fayrene
shouted into the world through the answering
machine over gunfire *I just want to make sure
yall's doing okay. I like the new lady friend.*
I like how she came in smilin' and huggin' and smilin'!
I like our boy's new lady friend!
We sat on the wavering stools.
When she finished and the machine clicked off
we held hands, bowed our heads, and your father
prayed loud not long.
And you said *Amen* and that you quite liked the new
lady friend too and no one laughed but me.

MYTHMAKING

Evening, your mother sat with your father
who took his breathing treatment. Clint Eastwood
ranged across the screen, music of gunshots and pounding.
You held my hand. We walked down the dirt lane.
We walked through birdsong, barn swallow, waxwing.
We passed the creek where you were Baptized.
Catbirds on the wire, two muscles bound of joy
and hunger. You said softly then, not the first time,
At our future event I imagine a toast.
The birds were bursting, the evening our idyll.
The gates of the cemetery were wide open
and we entered as innocents, identifying
tupelo, cowbird, the dark inversion
of swifts. When you led me to the family plot
how boldly we didn't consider, at our age,
combined age of one hundred and two, dying.
Even the soldier's grave,
alone, unwed, no parents, no children,
his low white stone at the top of the ridge,
bearing nothing, where you knelt alone, and closed
your eyes, did not seem to be a portent of the great depth
of what was not going to be our happiness.

ON COMING HOME ALONE TO A FLORIDA RINGNECK SNAKE ACROSS THE DOORSTEP

I know the red ring
means *puncture.*
I know common,
and know sliver, innocuous,
and blessing. I have to
get over you, Snake,
warming this way
in winter at my doorstep.
But I don't want to step over
even the smallest snake.
I don't want to open
my door, chance inviting him in.
I'm wearing a cotton skirt.
My head holds a full
day's heat, anger, longing
unwanted. I want warmth
too. Dear Unwound,
I could wear you out
as jewelry, as symbol, form you
into an obsidian brooch,
any letter: *S.*
Not for anything special.
Just out and about.
*Has that woman got a small
snake pinned to her blouse?*
Holy no. So *Punctatus punctatus,*
what am I to do with you?
How about tonight, I sleep
here at my doorstep. You go

inside, take my bed. You, take
my bed, curl on my white sheets.
I'll form myself into the crevice
between door and step
and draw my strength from here as you do,
muscle in the chasm.

FOR MY BIRTHDAY

My husband brought me a plastic container
that previously held arugula.
And he set it on its side
on our front step.
Thus he came seeming with nothing.
He did not look me
in the eye or pull me to him
but I did not yet understand.
I saw the future aged him in him and how
I would love his gray hair gone to white
and his age spots like syllables,
every souring molecule of him
so familiar to me from childhood.

My present was on the porch, he said after
dinner. I went outside and sat by the empty
plastic container, recycling in my mind.
Look closer, he said. Taped to the top
by its filament, a black thumb swung furiously.
He's not happy, he said. *He turned
dark on the way here.* I saw the gold
eye on the monarch chrysalis. I saw the wing
dots, gold, and veins, gold through the case.
I imagined the living juice turning into a bug.
Will we see him break through? I asked, wanting
so much to touch transformation.

In the morning, before work, I sat alone
on the front porch and wanted to hold her,
protect her, slow time down.
The ebony earring banged back and forth

so hard it tapped the plastic ceiling.
I watched for as long as I could.
When I got home that night,
a torn curtain of translucent lace hung
in the empty, fluttering.

POEM OF HIS MOTION

As a look first
he came to me
in a sunken living room,
among a syntax of grown-ups,
a poetry gathering, forest of garrulousness,
all of us trying to put into words
love of words and love of love and of woods, maybe
something of the heartbreak of living
or of awareness or not.
I wore a navy lace dress, black boots,
copper lipstick, headed somewhere after,
bent toward night.
I don't remember what I was up to.
Something with much less literacy.
Before the reading of the poems,
we were led to look at a painting
by the piano and he was close behind me
and close to me
when he whispered a secret.
I felt his breath in my ear and on my face,
a taste of warm, and male, and stale.
He was *looking*
at me, fox fiercely
out from under his rooftop
of dark gray. I drew in as I never do
when he saw me see and he
disappeared as a looker,
appeared as a slate:
I could write on him.
Then how *loving kindness* seemed to lower
his fine chin,

and lift his eyes as he saw
into me. This was
the animal moment.
I took him all in.
He moved in
with wild departures
then gone
in one liquid
movement.
Now alone
in my quiet rooms, I'm dumb-
struck by the power
of *wanted* wanting
to transform an entire state,
electrify a bower,
send a poet—forever—
to her alabaster (blank
page!) tower.

AFTER THE STORM

I walked out of my house across shining mud,
then through dull deeper mud, the lower
driveway a pond, the lawn all pond-under.
And in the dark standing water
at the garden gate, a million white quotation marks,
mosquito larvae punctuating disaster.
I found this good.
But the banyan was broken open, would never be right,
all its losses torn from the soft center—
now, too much light.
All the trees in my garden as dead branch
bowls now, empty-headed, open vases.
The back fence, blown away and I entered as a breeze
and knelt to find in a shadow on a stone:
an anole stabs a moth with a single claw.
Moth presses her wings to the stone,
trying to fly down but there's nowhere to go.
How did she come to be here, skewered
in this place after surviving the storm?
The lizard's yellow lipstick makes him look happy.
I tried to imagine when I would puncture
something so much larger than myself,
some thing that doesn't walk much or well but flies
and therefore seems, if not
capable of thought, an embodied thought.
Never. By the lawn chair, up-ended and slung
against the rubber tree, a blue jay
pierces the back of a slender anole who blushes browner brown,
the very late dark brown. The two of them stand there,
one paused, one dying.
I waded towards high ground,

hard mud and in a rush of fronds,
flushed a scruffy rabbit from the philodendron.
I smelled his sour fur. All the screaming
back here is silence. I'd come simply to see
what can't float. The old watering can can and when
I lifted it from the water the galvanized bucket swung heavy,
and the black snake spiraled up as though someone somewhere
was sing. She uncoiled before my eyes,
writing a great *S* and disappeared into mid-air.
Down with the watering can. Done with the inspection,
I walked back to the house in the wrong-hard sun.
This was our shade garden. This was our cocktail hour
and evensong, our easy and tended place, before the storm.
I walked past the moth, standing now on her legs,
her two hairs, her precarious last steps,
as the little dinosaur Rexed
his bug back down to the stone.
Past the blue jay who punched another
hole in the anole. Only I am empty-handed.
Should I have the rabbit by its neck?
The body of the snake in one hand, its head in
my mouth?

Inside, I stepped across the terrazzo floor
to the mudroom, where yet another lizard walks
with her high heel claw-feet across the great washing machine.
She waves her tiny front foot. *You must go.*
When I turned back, I saw across my floor
my footprints in mud, my walk across the garden
perfectly replicated on the terrazzo,
every step I've taken, in darkness, gleaming.

LEMON TREE

Across the street from my place
the abandoned house sinks
into pink sand, into bright.
One late afternoon—we were
new and it was just before the storm—
I led you through the side gate
past the crazy city of philodendrons
aching in low sun. Past the stump.
Meyer, the sweetest. Thin pale skins.
They're rotting on the ground,
you said of my bounty.
To touch one is to pick one—
each orb springs to the hand.
I pressed lemons into my blouse.
So many lemons, spotted
wild lemons, lemons with inner lives.
In my driveway you peeled
one perfect one. Their skins
tender, clear as ours. You gave it to me
to drink from and I sucked
the vibrant juice in and I bit
the silky flesh and handed the lemon
to you. And again. That sweet.

THE EVENING AFTER HE LEFT

I returned home from work and stood
alone in the darkest
room in the house in my blouse
and skirt, barefoot. I felt
the presence of a man
in the hallway. But I knew
no one was there.
I missed his long
talking. I missed praying
with him (though he did not
pray). I missed his
teeth, his lope, the him
of him. I missed the shadow
he left in his leaving.

I stood in the dark, barefoot
like a child. A river of light
came from the bedroom,
the prettiest room in the house.
I couldn't move my body.
I knew I did not need
to change to be less afraid.
I could see some new room
yet to be, beyond the pink light.
I sensed an orderly place.

In the dark inside the dark
in the kitchen,
I saw his cup, left behind
on the counter. The cup was
full of black liquid.

I placed my finger into his tea
still warm—not really warm
—to the touch. I drank.
I drank it all.

SELF-PORTRAIT BETWEEN
THE CLOCK AND THE BED

At last the end
of the great solitary
migration from the day
up into my head.
I stand in night, naked,
still, universal, arms hanging,
between the clock and the bed.
Here my body, covered in one
hundred and seventy-one
mosquito bites, must be
dabbed. A lingering cough.
My lover? Not loving. Not
certain. Not clear. Not here.
The salve? Clear. So, dab. I dab.
The clock shows an old time,
the bed a bright quilt,
the body, a strong girl who loves
her potatoes.
One of the legs, lonely. One
of the legs: solitude. I'm proud
of the quadriceps. *Sleep, horse.*
But I do not want to fold.
I do not want to go down.

After Edvard Munch

LONG TALKING

I am jealous of the parrots quilted on the tree in the alley behind your house, so many bright flights over you. I am jealous of your uncomfortable patio chairs, the iron table where you take your morning coffee, legs up. I am jealous of cream which swirls for you. You're about to go check your accounts, go for your noticing run. I'm jealous of my despair because it gets to be close to you. I'm jealous of your very successful butterfly garden. You are not even you and I'm jealous of my religion which knows this.

DEAR WOLF,

You were, you are
for a moment
an equation
I long
awaited
shiver = happiness /
man = interior access.
And the lexicon
of *hurt* in your fur
register
I translated
as *mirror*
and as *mine.*
Thus fluent
I thought
my sexy
diagnoses—
poor wolf,
also: *my friend*—
transformed
you as you appeared
at my table, howling,
such steadfast caroming!
I let you in
because you were
cold and alone.
But it wasn't musical notes
piercing my skin
after all. Hurt, hurt
alive, welted, I wept
when you said to me

I must hurt you to stay
warm inside,
to stay inside.

Now I walk
each day for clarity.
I know where you fold.
I go near but I no
longer call for you. The same
three choices in every fairy tale:
marry the man in the form
he's in or sleep
in a diaphanous dress.
Or walk alone toward
mystery, past
all known houses,
past filmy grounds and cemeteries
not knowing if another
will appear or if words
in a new language
will appear in their
little cloaks, their bright
little cloaks.

PRESENT STATE OF THE GARDEN

The bougainvillea he used to trim
snarls to thorns and its white
flowers, bracts—some leaves pretend
to be flowers—fall on the patio, melt in layers
of stain, first slippery, not safe. Now muck.
The loppers he closed over throats
of strands, rogues, and creepers, rusts
in the shed. His left-behind adze mildews
—iron and wood, militant pre-decay—
a tricky light coat of greening on his tool.
And cooch grass chokes the hawthorne to death.
Weeds knit themselves into the remnant
tapestry intent on takeover.
We'll keep you company, old girl.
They're already under and over
the fence. And the hedge, which lived as a line
of steady boxcars, steadfast perimeter,
a tribute not to tidiness but to love itself
as much more is required to make a good hedge
than simply containing by trimming back, withers.
A hedge is made of years and anticipation,
the marriage of patience and protection.
Now, abandoned, the windbreak bushes
into blunders and wild limbs, green vases.
I see more separations appear as patches.
How did he keep it so well? Before he left
everything was sturdy-seeming.
But the garden doesn't miss him. It thinks
it's beautiful and all intentions joy careening.

TWO MID-AFTERNOONS SIDE-BY-SIDE

1.

The ibis complete
their goosey pickering across the lawn.
I am not lonely even as light falls in veils.
The osprey return
to the pine with fish.
Their nest, a sprawling mess,
in the high boughs with two
homely chicks, open throats,
wanting, wanting, wanting.
Or is there just one great,
flustered singular wanting?

2.

The seed pearls on the new lemon tree
only shine in the afternoon.
The bells at St. Rafael's ring over
the water. *She's old* they peal
in monotone. She's an old teacher
and by Friday afternoon
even the banyan looks untutored,
musty and mottled and sad.
Evening, our great dark bay, holds
the beginning and the end, is hours away.
It is cold here even in the sun.

FEED THE SOIL

And then I did not weep
for weeks.
I drove across the long bridge,
listening. The water was black,
moonlight on the water, red.
I don't know why
I hurtled myself to the side
of the road on the causeway
and stood in the sand
at the head
of the bay. Sea grape
billows in towers here,
rooted in nothing.
I waded in.
The water was ice cold
as it never is.
I stood stock still ankle deep.
Like lava, the bay blistered
in the wolf moon light and wind.
And in every dark swell,
I saw menace
and more and it was mine.

PART II

AFTER

His departure, his books
between his legs, a bunch
of rejections. His winter
clothes still in my closet like old men
or moss. Strenuous biking.
It's been two months, eleven days.
Seven hours. He left *in the rain.*
Now sun pours down every day.
Letters from his mother. Her handwriting,
poetry. She prays, conquers cancers, deals
with his father who forgets he forgets.
She sent the photo of the small lamp her son—
still my husband, strange filament, gone out—
bought her for Christmas from Lowe's. With her.
I scour these details like a criminal.
Let me know all your news, Love.
When I read what she writes I write
him in my head, making him him again.
I think of lines from Sylvia Plath's letters
home to her mother. So much talk of batter!

I pretend things are mine. I want to take him
up on his former offer to love—
I mean to dig love— I mean to dig—
out the Brazilian pepper in the front garden.
My hacking has made everything come back
stronger, as he said it would.
The tree strangles the gardenia
upends the pavers, kills the lawn with its hungry roots.
Passersby duck now, bat my stalwart branchery.
He knew every part was poison. It's hard not to

over-identify with out-of-control things.
And there's the matter of his other offer
to repair the soft receptacle—the outdoor electrical outlet
behind lattice covered in jasmine, what a wicked place
for energy to come from,
so low and damp and constantly shocking
after the storm.

ACCIDENTAL PRACTITIONERS

In Wednesday night's class, the Introduction
to Forms & Techniques of Poetry, I'm teaching
as though we're on a small raft.
We are on a small raft.
We may never see the ones we love again.
Every poem is a message in a paper bottle.
Revision is urgency with tweezers.
How to pull out the bit not meant
to be there.
My brother died before midterm this term.
I have a student who has his name.
I call on this boy as often as I can.
I say his name aloud to alter
my relationship to grief.
I see you have your hand up, *Sean*.
I don't know if my brother ever read
a poem in his life. I worry I'm selling
poetry as salvation. Drinking and selling lines.
And in this same class I have a student
with my moved-out husband's name.
The husband student doesn't raise his hand, speak.
And in this same class, a student with my
father's name. He sleeps in the back row.
I do not call out his name. I don't want to wake him.
I do not put them in the same group.
I spread them around. I watch myself
closely: be very fair to the husband.
He's done nothing wrong. He got scared.
Of what? Garden light and dying and death.
Of what? The interior experience. Not well lit!
After the midterm, I imagine they'll be

back to themselves: the students will
manage their own independent identities.
Already things are settling.
But my bite is not correct.
I'm dubious about the last stanza.
I walk in the evenings alone. I bought
a linen dress with horizontal stripes.
I thought it would make me appear wider
in the sense of *unstoppable.*
But wearing stripes I just feel I'm in jail.
I read into all hours. I dread seeing him weave
through town, rooms with women, his looky look.
I know "love" when simplified to its lowest
common denominator means *sorrow*
tomorrow. I know it isn't too late to change.

Tonight I'm introducing the English sonnet
as a method for containing anxiety, grief's pulse.
We sit on the floor. We write by hand.
One hundred and forty syllables.
I call on my father. I call on my brother.
We write the sonnets as letters
to the ones we have lost. I have never lost
anyone, my husband-student says,
out of the blue.
You can lose me, I tell him.
Pretend you will lose me.

AFTER OFFICE HOURS, AFTER EPIPHANY
AND THOSE BEAUTIFUL WORDS *DEAR FRIEND*

for Elaine Sexton

Mary is dropping out of the writing program.
Last semester she hallowed her body,
her slacks exclamation points,
her slenderness witness, her less more and more dangerous,
so much of her gone, moving headlong toward nothing.
Over break, she dyed her long dark hair purple,
increasing the stringiness of everything.
I like your hair, girls in our class said before class.
Meaning *Mary, come back.* Meaning
Mary we still see you.
Did she need someone to say
I am profoundly missing you?
Can this be said with words?
I don't know. She wrote poems
about her attempts to convert in Kissimmee,
her boyfriend devout not devoted.

I know a lot my students do not know.
I know mutability.
A kind of terrible wolfing.
If students could walk behind their teachers
through any one day and one night
what could they taste and see?

My old teacher Gordon turns 98 next week.
Can you believe it? he says. He calls me to read sacred
words aloud every Thursday at seven p.m.

We read one sentence at a time.
Tonight: *The light of the body is the eye.*
At Hope, I dreaded church with students—
the God I love as a lover I love in privacy.
But here in the secular swamps of Tampa
at the state university, I am proselytizing.
I kneel in my office and pray before classes.
I want to kneel beside Mary.
I want to translate for her and with her the lilies.
I want to demonstrate girls' tears, Mary,
are the same expression of Divine as the vine's
quiet, steady blossoms. They will not last.
And they're meant to last and last.
Don't disappear. Follow me.

But violent disappearances are taking place.
Thank God here comes the evening
mail, thick with a packet of my friend's poems.
Among the fliers, her rowboat and coast,
her beloved brother dead,
her former lover, dying. Her therapist said
It doesn't matter. My friend painted those words
on her bedroom wall. *It doesn't matter.*
She stitched those words in needlepoint,
wrote them in the snow, sang them in sorrow
and celebration. *It doesn't matter. It doesn't matter.*
And she made us all cards, fretful steady fonts.

INVENTORY FOR A PEDAGOGY AT MIDLIFE

I carry few things not made
of paper: carrots, an apple,
my cannon of hot tea
on which I've scratched an *H*.

I walk into the classroom
carrying a tower of poems
begging my students to silence
their phones. *Come alive!*

Every breath rhymes.
Every breath rhymes.
We make contact. I bring
them syllables.

Outside the classroom I'm afraid.
We're afraid. I carry books
into my bed. I sleep naked with books.
No one knows how to live alone.

after Gunter Eich

AFTER CLASS

I stay up late watching a strange
program, a nurse addicted to pills
who rescues weak non-angels in her city,
studies her daughters like
molecule experiments. Too late.
I'm not going to have children.
In the office, I'm bleary; the ladies
toilet has a sign—we aren't flushing
properly. More has to happen with
the handle. I sit. I blot. Susanna calls
me into her office: she's seven
weeks pregnant! I go to class with
a wand. The secretary has designed this
as a Harry Potter theme week—I don't know
the books, the little wizard, but I know
how to play a game. My wand is a stick
from the lawn but I tap heads,
point at chalk, open the door. *Quit
college,* I tell my students. Wand
wave. *I'll sign your drop slips!*
Be poets. You're that good. And it's true.
Their genius has put me under
a spell. They laugh: they don't know
what's true. I do.

Drive home after, too tired to eat, eat olives,
too many. Drive fast, late to Pilates, which
I can perform in work clothes, a skirt and tights.
I tell my teacher I might cry on the mat:
John, my friend, is entering hospice.
Then your body really needs this today,

she says. I press myself down. I make
myself into a slice of toast. I balance
on my hip bones—hawk. I scoop.
I fly over the ground. I grab my
mouse. I fling the mouse. Over and over,
I fake fly. But the ground, it pulls so hard.
Is death simply a magnet in the core
and not to be feared—it's just energy?
The unending losses—they've not yet even begun.

ELEGY WITH PLANT-SITTER

Susanna comes by my house. We hug in
my driveway, evensong as summer dresses.
She's here to return my peace lily
and the lobelia. She pulls plants
out of the bottom shelf of her stroller,
voila, foliage! The baby hands me
his top-shelf foot. I want to
put it in my mouth. He smiles,
wise. He's glad I'm not
his mother. I would eat him, then fall
into a Frank O'Hara poem-lifestyle,
walk around at lunchtime,
a nip in my pocket, wanting to be rich,
follow around my student who writes
better than you know who.
Poor little baby. Eaten, then by himself forever.
Now, in his stroller, under the summer
evening sky, low as mattresses, he hollers.
Loud. Yes, he's gotten very loud,
Susanna says, all balm. She leans down,
speaks softly to her baby. I see they are
such good friends, among
other things. She finishes his thought,
he finishes her mouth.
After she leaves, I carry the plants inside,
set them on my counter.
These plants were the two plants
I received when my father died,
one from my aunt and one from my ex.
What am I keeping alive?

MY STRUGGLE

For marina. For bay. Against rising sea. For lochs. For love. For a twin, for a hold, for a living. Against cane. Against drink. For memory. For complexity. For heat. Against "characters." For clarity. For religious practice. For religious lying down on ground. Against looseness. Against the best against the worst. Against pretty. For dun with small eyes. For self. For no-self. Against travel. For trains. For weirdness. For ghosty. For hush. For pointless. For disciples. Against disciples. Against evening. For a family. Against a family. For the reliable moon, reliable in its come and go against the obliterating sun. Against one. For salt. For frond. For linen. Against musical silences. For girls' voices. Against your not being here. For we should not be so solitary this close to the sea.

AFTER MY MOTHER DIED

She slept in my bone body for a year.
My missing her a lonely hush. My grief
a gold thing I carried as an immanence.
And then she woke up and I came back from the dead
to find her driving various cars, in many thin blue old women,
bent, intent on low tasks, retrieving
what they've dropped, turning down an aisle in Publix
with a certain hesitation in their gait, holding
tight the cart. Holding tight. I see her in the evenings
in the wispy crones at the park.
I see her cowering on the church steps
where wrung-out ancient women sleep
on black plastic sheeting supplied by the city.
I want to bring one of these women home.
What if I did. I don't know what is mine
and what is hers and what is the grief of living.

Volatile Irish skin, remarkably thick hair everywhere,
high arches, low blood sugar, prone to night terror,
        penchant for lemon,
bicycles—I'm her and not her and faded her.
Did she give me religious life,
a sanctified touch of her touched? I do not see
the saints as she did, marauders in our rooms, or hear
commanding demons but the pure presence of
God does join me to this world. And I hear her voice now.
I hear her whispering. She touches. I'm touched.
As a girl, I fought her to the ground.
I fought as snake fights bird.

She writes on my body now
with her veins. She pulses under my skin,
blue and visible. *Her* gnarly fingers on my keyboard.
Her liver-spotted hands on my steering wheel.
Her white, wild hair—that nest—mine.
I pull strands from the hairbrush,
set them outside my door
to keep snakes away.

MY MOTHER IN MY BED

I wear her Victorian
nightgown winter nights. Last night

she wore hers in my dream. We didn't touch
but she was close, warm and bright

as never in real life.
We watched each other watch

The Great British Baking Show.
When I was young

she made many difficult desserts.
In the dream, we worried for the sweetness

in each contestant's yearning. Together
we predicted every dough disaster.

And I was my small self
in search of small things.

COLOR RECOLLECTION

The touch of terrazzo, white ground
flecked with a million marble
chips black turquoise cream silver bits
as independent and orchestrated
as syllables. How I crept, not yet
a walker, across ice flooring, memorizing
shapes of all the shapes, reading the world
of separate pieces as families
in the matrix of relationship.
First touch, my silk
quilt. First taste, the chewy corner
of my silk quilt. Second taste
of taste, my father's acrid metal
beer can, the lapel of sharper metal,
sour cold too cold liquid,
rottenness liquefied to gold.
To touch the grass and feel cut
over my whole body, tiny red slits.
To separate the thick rough blades
and burrow down into the brain
of the grass. The world roiling under
thatch mattedness, the white worms,
obsidian bugs, transparent feelers,
their pulsing larvae
like pearls. The hedge a tower.
The dead baby bird warm.
Smell of sweet death. The burning
of the orange picked from the small greening
Valencia struggling outside my bedroom window,
My lips on fire still on fire.

THINGS I AM SURPRISED I LOVE

New pillow of my belly in my hands,
more of me, suddenly lush at midlife, this blossoming
a peachy doughy lover
I carry somewhat secretly under my tunic
like a baby, not like a baby,
my gorgeous solitude amplified.

Raw Brussel sprout
I pick off the kitchen floor.
I put it in my mouth and see
so much more is on the floor
than I understood.
The desiccated chaos of my living.
Outside the window, a flicker on the birdbath
with two berries, washing each.

The wrack of the garden
to the west where
I never go, Queen Anne's lace
high as the house, torpedo grass dactyls,
the unbeatable cacophony of weed green
lazy chaos.

A line of hard black
ants on the window sill
creating a sentence of all punctuation
which makes meaning all morning.

Bursts of cold wind in the living room,
invisible chill bulleting through gaps
in the doors and windows, force

I'll use to harden myself
for something painful later.

Sand in the house
which makes me feel unexpectedly
part of a gritty prediction:
the human experience
just before fossildom.

Without playing, deleting
some of the messages left by my former husband
not knowing what I'm losing, sweetness or anger
not knowing what I'm saving, gentle inquiry or silence.

The fact I left outside
during what's supposed to be
dry season
my bicycle rusting,
handlebars dripping,
hibiscus petals translucent
on the seat,
on the patio
in the rain.

after Nazim Hikmet

POOR SWIMMERS

1.

My friend's daughter swims
in a salt water swimming pool.
"It tastes like tears."
She complains.
She refuses to leave
the pool. "That water was
someone's tears
and I was just getting
used to it."

2.

At the graveyard in my town
I don't know
a soul. I walk there pretending
I'm comfortable
with the dead floating
in dirt. This morning,
a rickety funeral,
elderly leaning forward,
straining in the sun.
A loose child stomped towards
a fresh pit by the back fence
and she mimed a swan dive
at the foot of the grave.

FROM MICHIGAN ON HER WINTER BREAK, MY NIECE

Lays out on my driveway, flattened
by the sun in her mirrored sunglasses,

motionless as though prepped for surgery,
her toenails blue, her body washed up

to my doorstep in need of a solution
for life. *I'm not me,* she said last night.

I didn't tell her I'm not me either.
Do I look different? she wants to know, inside

after sunning as she presses her skin,
hoping anything under pressure might be our proof.

ON A RAINY AFTERNOON IN DECEMBER

My niece and I walked along the water—white pelicans, night heron,
glorious bunches of pink wings poking out of Bird Island,

the mangrove rookery appearing in the mist
as a cake laced with satin feathers, beak and claw.

Now she sits atop the guest bed—her nest, she calls it—Instagramming
    raindrops
on palm fronds out her window. We live in a silent painting.
    Girls without mothers.

I miss him. She misses her him. Love's a lens
to see the both at once: the bright world and the bottom of the sea.

On the fourth day through greasy rain we made our way to the museum,
where she loved a female nude made out of sky and I a canvas keyhole.

When we stood at last in the grand finale, the splashy
chamber at the end of the exhibition, streamy white clouds

were projected on "real" blue skies—the floor all sky, walls sky—and cotton
clouds hung from the ceilings like bursts of *hahahaha*. We videoed

each other videoing each other against the wind-swept cloud-image screens,
and for the first time in a long time I felt real.

MEETING MY EIGHTY-YEAR-OLD AUNT AT THE FOUNTAIN OF YOUTH IN ST. AUGUSTINE FOR LUNCH

In the courtyard with lemon trees
and the fountain she rises slowly,
so slowly. From where I'm standing, she appears to rise
from the water, and her beauty ranges over
the tiles, her lipstick slipping, her perfume
our mysterious mist.
We embrace arranging our pale bones
cautiously as though I'm a dove and she's
a dove. *Don't get old alone,*
she whispers into my hair.
Her new boyfriend, sixty, well,
sixty-*something* takes our
photograph by the fountain.
She wants to know the condition
of my heart. It's not too soon,
she says, to find a new lover.
She scares them off, her boyfriend says,
Can see that by looking at her.
I look him in the eye. I don't think
he's scared off.
My aunt and I hold hands.
I'm open, I say. I am open.
My aunt takes off her ring,
puts it on my finger. *Something sparkly.*
She shines as a child.
Here's lunch. Soup and the famous
salad, white wine and shrimps,
and then, while we are waiting

for the coffees to come, she wanders
over to the well and
she reaches, I think she thinks
unseen, her fingertips
into the cool water.

BEAUTY

Do you want to go back
inside? the neighbor asks
his small dun dog. *Beauty,*
do you want to go inside?
A long look at the tiny fluff,
as if speech is imminent.
As if anything is imminent.

What would help you
unpack the boxes?
Love. And I want an authentic
relationship with unruliness,
layers, and with inside
the dark known unknown.
Even though it's a cathedral,
I've avoided this ugly place,
passed by every day.
After the session I go inside
St. Marks, finally, the concrete block
church like a warehouse surrounded
by run-off ponds on the low side
of the highway.

A woman named Mary
works in the office. She shines
lay minister shine. I hold her hands
in mine as she holds my hands
in hers: bone, vein, one pulse.
I'm not a hand-holder—this drawing
together is a mystery. She lists
the ministries: tending and dying.

How about a tour? Food pantry, so full.
Cradles line the hallway. Candlelight
in every room and faded daylight.
She calls the crumbling patio *the piazza*.
Piazza! But when I look, I see
together, here, we're inside and outside.
It's not hideous. A concrete stamp
on Florida. Yes. It's a piazza.

INTERSTATE FOUR ODE

In October,
I drive into the city for a party
at the museum and I am
pulled down by the highway
by a power moon, windows down,
Latin chant on the stereo,
evening sky so soft evening
enters my car and the liquid humid
skim coats my skin. Florida
has the atmosphere of another
planet. The moon tonight
is the same width as Earth and it's a long drive
from childhood to the art museum
or to anywhere at all.
When I was a girl, this was a two lane
road. I rode in the family car alone
in the world of the back seat.
I counted telephone poles
and other rhythmic talismans.
That's how hope is known,
held by fingertips, by counting
simple things that repeat.
An eight-lane highway now. I drive
past newly imported palm trees planted
alongside the highway
and like these inexpensive exclamation
points, I am returned to this place
I'm originally from. I know more trees
here than I do people.
The swamps glisten. I glisten back
and drive towards moon.

We call the Harvest Moon
Orange Popsicle Moon.
I am so lonely for weather
that makes you want
to put on clothes. I drive past
trailer parks and drainage
ditches, long gully stitches, frontage
lanes of my old neighborhood.
I can hear the pop.
I feel my father's breath.
When I pass Dinosaur World,
cut-out plywood brontosauruses
along a thin wood fence.
I realize I've driven almost
fifty miles in the wrong direction,
toward the house where I was born.
I loop around, and take a moment
with the faded dinos.
I knew them way back when,
when real was real.
I remember my father peeing here
next to our beige Plymouth wagon,
broad daylight. I remember my mother's
shame.
Good-bye Dinosaur World.
Good-bye miles of RV World.
The moon's paler, smaller, behind me now.

When I arrive at the museum
women in black dresses
scatter on the lanai, batting mosquitoes,
drinking white wine from foam cups.

A tall man plays xylophone.
Inside, a couple is dancing on the marble.
I lean over the balcony to watch a small girl
run in circles on the lawn
that slides down to meet the black river.

EVENING DURING A LONG ILLNESS

1.

I carry a cup of tea into the garden. Really
I carry nothing. A little thirst. St. Augustine
grass a patch the size of a king bed—
is it even a garden? Kleenexes
of gardenia blossoms dropped on the splinters
of grub-gray lawn. Thus, the dry blades
imitate a little haven. Along the fence, frangipani,
jasmine in full bower—I'd tell you all
about the perfume on my skin, the aura
of glory here, my hair, but weeks ago the virus
snuffed my sense of taste, all scents.
I wonder what will return when it returns.
Part of me imagines youth coming back
with what I think of as *my* health.
The heart of hope: better will be *better*.
Dizzy, I step through the gate,
I lower my body, odalisque the old girl very
alive deep inside this pale soft still-breathing
length of skin-on-skeleton—imagine a kind of downed
arrow, a broken kite—over the bright blue
Sunbrella bolster purchased long ago
from the barn of pottery or the elm of
west, somewhere far, far from this place,
a low isle off the Florida peninsula,
this state that hangs on, for now,
bobbing,
as it sinks slowly into the dull warm blue sea.
I too sink here on the grass,
I breathe below
sea level, below industry,

below thought, breathe
half-sunk air somehow
into my damp self, while holding
the shallow water in the bay at bay
with my breath.

2.
With every breath
these evenings I'm breathing underwater.
I dwell in the cellophane slip between
enlightenment and reincarnation.
It's a low place.
I don't really want to go anywhere ever again.
Draped on the pavers in the garden,
flung thing, in a nightgown—
my dead mother's white lawn high-neck Victorian—
I always feel stranded in a nightgown,
dramatic and fragile, part girl and part her:
my bone-thin sweet, grim mother.
I'm ancient, too: a kind of poetic cotton warning.
Tonight, the gown is damp, the lawn parched,
and I've been without company
for two months, so the plastic bag drifting
about in the breeze on the grass seems to
want to know me, seems to have something
to say to me. And I to it!
Come closer, CVS bag, I love you!
I want to be touched by something, any
alive presence, any evidence of breath.
Down the bricks the bag disappears, to the bay
into the ocean to impersonate a jellyfish.
Inside, later, I will measure oxygen

in my body with a drugstore oximeter:
not enough.
And when I sleep, now I dream I cannot measure
oxygen in the sea of red water,
not enough, not enough. I wake, over and over,
as struggle, wet thrash.

But now, fading with the light on the patio,
I roll on my back. An alligator-spider web
strung from silky guy wires, ties the garden gate
to the bougainvillea and I see the dark knot
at the center, tiny papoose in the heart of the web,
wavering, struggling to be free, encased in filament
black glimmer glass. I sense my delicate bones
on the pavers, and where my feathers used to be
but never really were, now stabbing me,
my perforated lungs. I see I need to shave my legs.

And that's how I remember the book
I wrote and illustrated when I was a girl.
Somehow, I have it to this day, encased
in glassine, locked in a file drawer,
just there, steps away, in my pink house below
sea level, the story of a young furred creature
who has on her own built a home
of branches and spider-web windows on the river
—it's a dam. And the creature, Little Fur, searches
on land, all the forest wide, calling for her mother
who will never reappear.
So many steps away.